THE 12 B
IN THE LAKE DISTRICT

PAUL BUTTLE

Published by
AMADORN

Acknowledgement

I would especially like to thank George Minter, without whose practical help this guide would never have been produced.

First published July, 1988
Reprinted August, 1988, February, 1989, October, 1989, April, 1991
February, 1992, October, 1992, May, 1993, May, 1994, May, 1995, February, 1997
July 1998

ISBN 0 9513717 0 3

Published by Amadorn, 18 Brewery Lane, Keswick, Cumbria.
Printed by Nuffield Press, Abingdon.

CONTENTS

INTRODUCTION

The purpose of this brief guide is to help the experienced or aspiring hillwalker with only a limited knowledge of the area to obtain the fullest enjoyment possible from their visits to the Lakeland fells. Essentially therefore this is a guide explaining where to begin.

The title of this guide is a little presumptious; the walks described are of course my own opinion of the twelve best walks in the Lake District. However there is nothing unique about this selection. Nearly all the walks are established routes and anyone with a good knowledge of the Lake District would probably compile a very similar list. I have made the selection using three basic guidelines:

Each walk should be circular.

Each walk should be a full-day's walk.

None of the walks should overlap.

I have chosen a selection of circular walks because although I have been careful to think of people like myself who are dependent on public transport I have assumed that most people using this guide will have their own transport, and will therefore want to return to the starting point of a walk having first arrived there by car. I do in fact believe that some walks can be bettered by using public transport and by making them linear rather than circular walks, and I hope in the future to produce another guide describing such walks, but in this guide I have restricted myself to describing circular routes.

Each of the walks is a full-day walk as quite simply full-day walks are more satisfying than half-day or shorter walks. I have more to say on the timing of walks below but essentially each walk should occupy most walkers between the time they finish a leisurely holiday breakfast and the time they sit down to a welcome evening meal. All the walks therefore are fairly substantial fell walks.

Deciding that none of the walks should overlap not only makes the choice of walks a little easier, but also helps to make this a better overall guide to the Lake District. Therefore anyone completing all the walks described in this guide should gain quite a good knowledge of the Cumbrian Fells.

I have attempted to make this guide as concise as possible, so that it can be quickly and readily assimilated. On the whole route-finding on the fells is not difficult, at least when not in mist. Many people will be able to follow the walks by just referring to the sketch maps. In many instances the direction notes are hardly needed. Even so I hope they will be referred to as hopefully there is at least one direction note, if not more, in each walk description which greatly assists the task of route-finding, and makes this guide worthwhile.

I have not sought to justify any particular route, or to explain why I have gone this way round or taken this particular approach rather than another. Lack of space precludes me from explaining these points. Having had over twenty years experience of fellwalking in the Lake District I hope the user will place some faith in my view that these are the best walks he or she can first choose to accomplish.

Choice of maps

Though a great deal of care has been taken in producing the sketch maps used in this guide they are not intended to be a substitute for the Ordnance Survey maps of the Lake District which are really an essential requirement for walking on the Lakeland hills. I particularly recommend the use of the Ordnance Survey 1″ Tourist map of the area. Not only does this map cover all the walks described in this guide, but also as the sketch maps are drawn on the same scale the user will find it easier to relate the information shown on the sketch maps to this particular map.

Timing of Walks

It is not possible to give a precise time for each of the walks, as much will depend on the fitness of the individual and the weather conditions prevailing at the time. In addition much will also depend on how much time you tend to spend admiring the scenery. Therefore I have suggested an "average time" for each walk, allowing one hour for every thousand feet of ascent and one hour for every three miles of distance, this being a more generous adaptation of a rule known as Naismith's Rule. A very fit person will be able to complete the walks in faster times than the times calculated on this basis, whereas a novice hillwalker might easily take two hours longer. The "average time" therefore can only be used as a rough guide to the length of time a walk might take, and should be adapted according to your own experience.

Public Transport

Information on the public transport system in the Lake District can be found at the end of the book on page 32.

Go n-éirí an bóthar leat.
Tá mé ag dul go dtí an teach tábhairne!

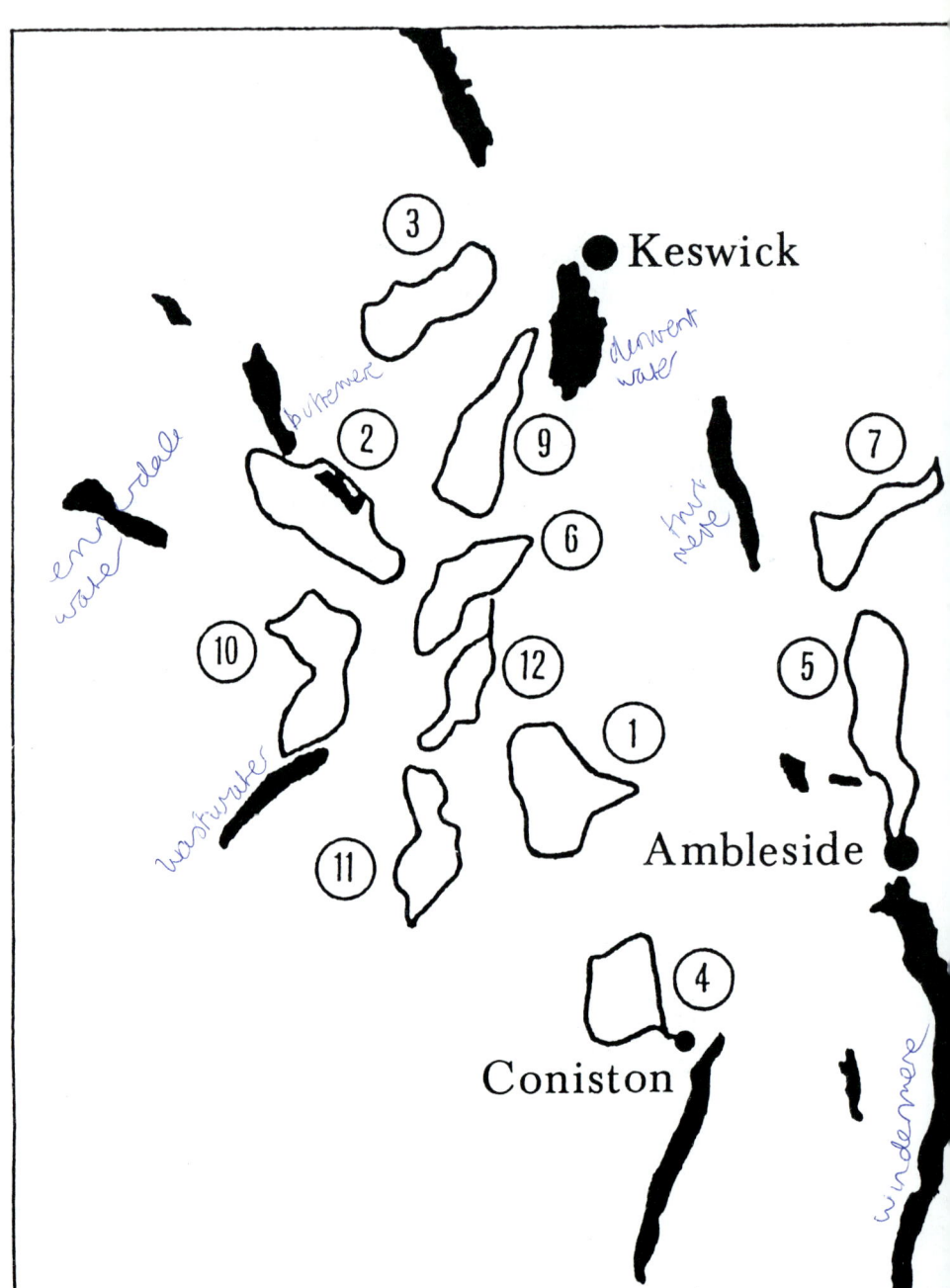

Keswick

Coniston

Ambleside

③ ② ⑨ ⑦ ⑥ ⑩ ⑫ ⑤ ① ⑪ ④

ennerdale water

buttermere

derwent water

thirlmere

wastwater

windermere

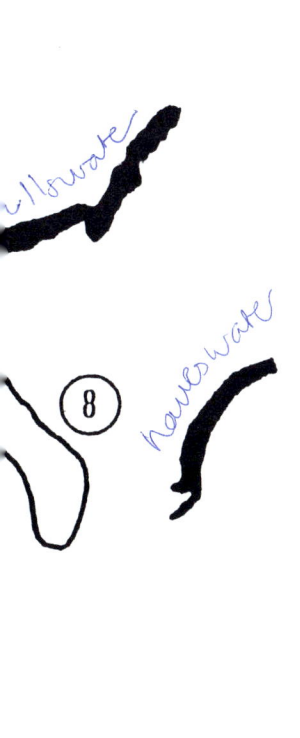

1 Bowfell and Crinkle Crags

2 The Buttermere Fells

3 The Coledale Horseshoe

4 The Coniston Fells

5 The Fairfield Horseshoe

6 Great Gable

7 Helvellyn

8 High Street

9 The Newlands Horseshoe

10 Pillar

11 Scafell

12 Scafell Pike

BOWFELL 2,960 feet & CRINKLE CRAGS 2,816 feet

Distance	8½ miles
Total Ascent	3,500 feet
Average Time	6½ hours
Starting Point	*Old Dungeon Ghyll Hotel* (NY 286 061). Car park next to hotel.
Public Transport	Bus. Ambleside to the Old Dungeon Ghyll Hotel. Service 516. Operators Cumberland.

Crinkle Crags is so called because of the nature of its skyline. It is a complex rocky ridge, changing all the time as you round each successive rocky knoll. By contrast Bowfell is more straight forward, with the lines of the fell sweeping up to a distinctive peak, from which eastwards can be surveyed the whole of Langdale, and away to the west the Scafells.

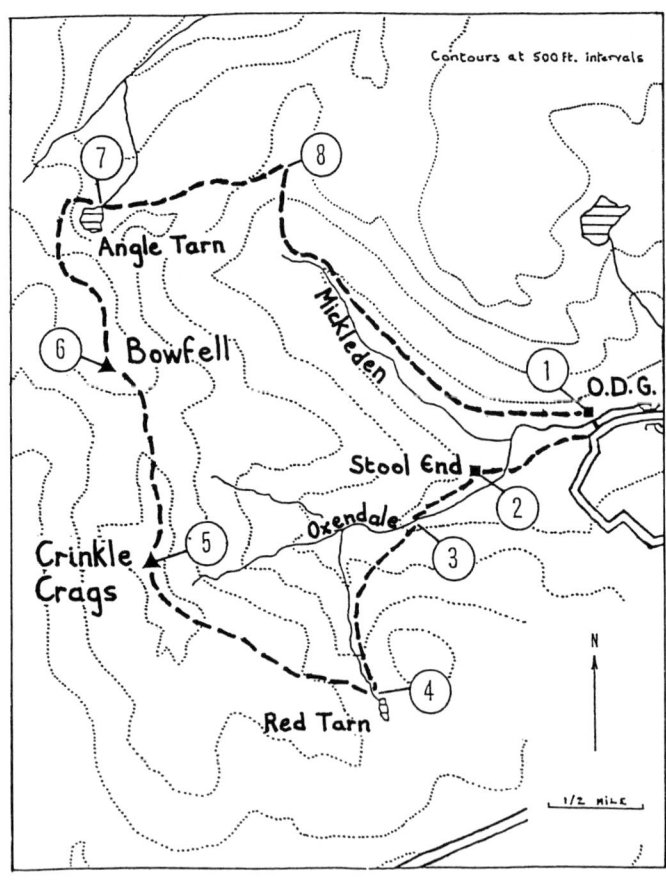

1   Exit from the Old Dungeon Ghyll Hotel car park and turn right. The road soon turns sharp left but straight ahead next to a red letter box is a six bar farm gate. Continue through this gate along a surfaced access road to Stool End Farm. (¾ mile)

2   Pass through a small gateway next to the gable end of the farm house and bear left along an obvious path following the side of the wall and leading into Oxendale. Walk a short way along the valley to a narrow single beamed footbridge crossing over Oxendale Beck. (½ mile)

3   Cross over the footbridge and continue along the path on the other side which soon begins making a steep ascent up to Red Tarn. Just before reaching Red Tarn the ground levels and a distinct path crosses over Brown Gill, the beck flowing from Red Tarn. (1 mile)

4   Cross over Brown Gill and continue on the path climbing between Great Knott and Cold Pike on to Crinkle Crags. Between the first "crinkle" and the second "crinkle" there is a distinct gap from which a path ascends a small gully to reach the summit of the fell. This route involves a small climb of about 7 foot known as "Bad Step". This is not difficult but can be avoided if necessary by moving left from the base of the gully and taking a curved shaped route of ascent to the top. (1¾ miles)

5   From the highest point on Crinkle Crags move northwards along the ridge descending to "Three Tarns", from which a very visible path climbs up to the summit of Bowfell. (1¼ miles)

6   From the summit of Bowfell a path descends northwards to Ore Gap, and then from Ore Gap to Angle Tarn. As you descend down to Angle Tarn note the path leading away from the outflow of the tarn north-east wards to Stake Pass. (1 mile)

7   From Angle Tarn take the path described above leading to Stake Pass. A hundred yards from the tarn another path veers off to the right towards a distinctive boulder. This path is so indistinct that to begin with you may doubt its validity, but after a hundred yards or so it becomes more evident. It leads to a small gap between Rossett Crag and Black Crags overlooking Mickleden from which a delicate cairned path descends diagonally down to the left some few hundred feet to meet up with the former packhorse route leading down from Stake Pass. (1 mile)

8   Follow the old packhorse route down in to Mickleden and along the valley floor back to the Old Dungeon Ghyll Hotel. (2¼ miles)

THE BUTTERMERE FELLS

Highest Point	High Stile 2,644 feet
Distance	10 miles
Total Ascent	3,100 feet
Average Time	6½ hours
Starting Point	*Buttermere Village Car Park* (NY 175 169).
Public Transport	Minibus. Keswick to Buttermere. Operators Cumberland. Seasonal only.

The Buttermere Fells, Red Pike, High Stile and High Crag form one of the finest ridge walks in the Lake District. The approach taken in this walk via Scale Force is not as steep and arduous as the the more direct route from Buttermere via Bleaberry Tarn, nor is it as busy. It moves up through a fellside of heather which is a pleasing contrast to the ridge proper. After the ridge, and the descent to Scarth Gap, the pull up to Hay Stacks is arduous, but is totally rewarding. The route over Hay Stacks is full of interest. The final miles of the walk follow the peaceful shores of Buttermere lake, from where you can look up and admire those fells over which you were crossing but a few hours before.

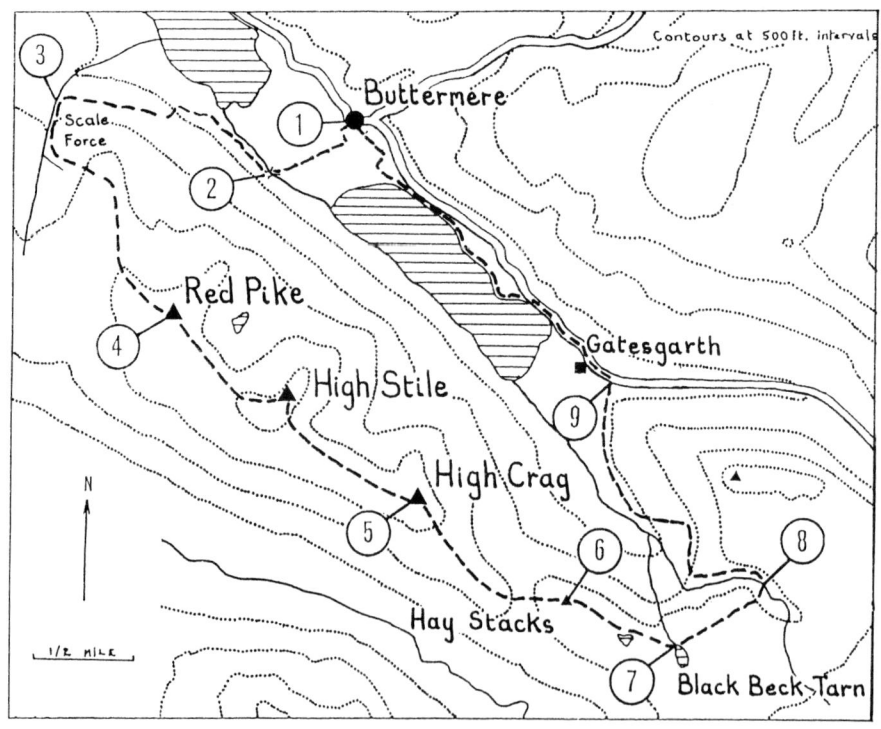

1   From Buttermere village follow an obvious trackway to the left of the Fish Hotel leading past the bar of the hotel sign posted as leading to Buttermere lake and Scale Bridge for roughly one hundred yards until you come to a kissing gate on your right at a bend in the trackway. Pass through the gate and proceed along another trackway to Scale Bridge. (½ mile)

2   Cross over the bridge and follow an obvious path heading towards Crummock Water which soon curves westwards away from the lake towards Scale Force. ¾ mile from the bridge the path turns sharp left and climbs uphill for a hundred yards and then turns sharp right to avoid a section of bog. This presents the only difficulty in following the path which is otherwise quite clear on the ground. Despite the path's obvious appearance on the ground it is only represented on the 25,000 scale map as a faint black dashed line. (1¼ miles)

3   To the left of the ravine containing the waterfall of Scale Force is a steep worn reddish path. This leads to the top of the falls where it continues along Scale Beck and then veers off to the left initially following a small tributary of Scale Beck up to Ling Comb Edge which it follows to the summit of Red Pike. (1½ miles)

4   Continue along the ridge to High Stile and then on to High Crag. (1½ miles)

5   From High Crag there is a steep descent of 900 feet to Scarth Gap. Cross over the Gap and continue on up to Hay Stacks. (1 mile)

6   An obvious path continues over Hay Stacks eventually reaching Black Beck Tarn. (½ mile)

7   Cross over the outflow from Black Beck Tarn and continue along another obvious path leading north-easterly, weaving around some attractive knolls and crags and then descending down to a distinctive beck flowing towards Buttermere. (½ mile)

8   Cross over the beck and follow the path immediately to your left that contours above the stream to link up with a constructed path leading westwards down into the valley which was originally built for the purpose of transporting slate from Dubs Quarry. Follow this path down to the roadway at Gatesgarth. (1½ miles)

9   Continue along the road to where it meets the north east corner of the lake. From this point a sign-posted path follows the lake shore back to Buttermere village. (1¾ miles)

THE COLEDALE HORSESHOE

Highest Point	Crag Hill 2,753 feet
Distance	9 miles
Total Ascent	3,700 feet
Average Time	6 1/2 hours
Starting Point	*Braithwaite* (NY 232 236). Car parking is possible near to the school in the centre of the village.
Public Transport	Bus. Keswick to Braithwaite. Service X5. Operators Cumberland,

This walk takes in five peaks that surround Coledale Beck. Without too much extra effort it is possible to include Grasmoor, Outside, Stile End, Scar Crags and Causey Pike - ten peaks altogether, a peak bagger's dream. Although this walk involves more climbing than any other walk in this guide, and would be over four and a half thousand feet if all the peaks mentioned were included, in doing this walk I have never had the sense of ascending all those feet, and was surprised to learn how many there were. More rounded than other Lakeland hills, as they are formed of Skiddaw Slate, and not as rugged, the Coledale Hills are perhaps less taxing than their heights suggest.

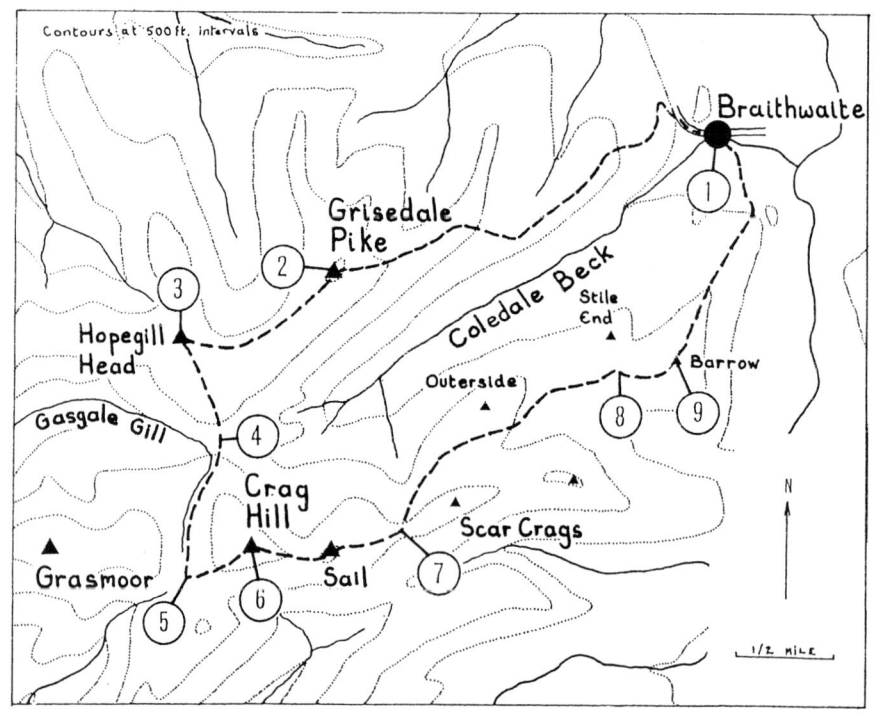

1   Walk out of the village uphill along the B5292 to Whinlatter. A quarter of a mile from the village on your left is a small car park sited in a former quarry. Follow the path starting from the car park sign posted as leading to Grisedale Pike. This is a very steep climb to begin with to the top of Kinn, followed by a welcome level section, followed by another steep climb to the summit of Grisedale Pike itself. (2½ miles)

2   Moving S.W. follow the ridge to Hopegill Head, first crossing over an unnamed miniature peak and then descending some 300 feet followed by an almost equal ascent. (1 mile)

3   From Hopegill Head cross over a slight depression to the top of Sand Hill and then descend southwards to Coledale Hause, the saddle between Hopegill Head and Eel Crags. (¾ mile)

4   From the Hause follow the path up stream along the upper section of Gasgale Gill which flows from the col between Grasmoor and Crag Hill to the top of the col itself. (½ mile)
    (From this point it is possible to include the summit of Grasmoor, well worth doing so for the views down on to Crummock Water, by taking the path to your right leading westwards to the summit, and then returning back to the col. Should you do so this will add another 400 feet of ascent and 1½ miles to the circuit. Allow ¾ hour.)

5   From the very top of the col on your left is a distinct path leading N.E. to the summit of Crag Hill. (¼ mile)

6   Moving eastwards from the summit there is first a steep descent then a shorter climb to the top of Sail, followed by a more gradual descent to the col between Sail and Scar Crags. (¾ mile)

7   From the col take a distinctive path descending from the ridge to the N.E. A mile from the col, just after passing Outerside on your left, notice another thinner path branching off to the left from the path you are on and clearly contouring to Barrow Door, the gap between Stile End and Barrow. (1½ miles)

8   From Barrow Door follow the path to the summit of Barrow. (¼ mile)

9   From the summit of Barrow descend the rather gentle ridge leading back to Braithwaite village. (1¼ miles)

THE CONISTON FELLS

Highest Point	The Old Man of Coniston 2,631 feet
Distance	7½ miles
Total Ascent	3,500 feet
Average Time	6 hours
Starting Point	*Coniston* (SD 302 976). A car park is sited in the centre of the village.
Public Transport	Bus. Ambleside to Coniston. Service 505. Operators Cumberland.

This walk is a circuit of the fells which provide a dramatic setting to the village of Coniston as viewed from the lake. Being in the Furness area these fells were recently part of Lancashire, before the creation of Cumbria, consequently the Old Man of Coniston was once the highest point in Lancashire. Yet Swirl How, a mile and a half away, stands only one foot lower. It is perhaps as well that their respective heights are not reversed, or else the numbers now content with only ascending the Old Man would be thronging the ridge to Swirl How.

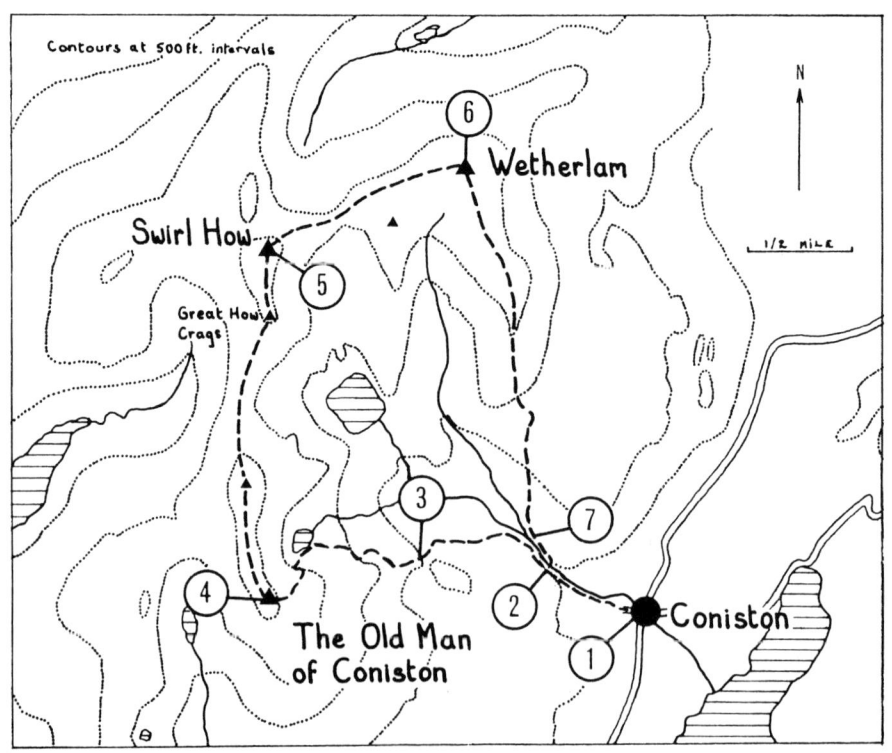

1   Starting from the bridge in the centre of the village next to Barclay's bank follow the road sign posted as leading to the Sun Hotel 150 yards. Turn right at the gable end of the hotel up a short access road sign posted as leading to the Old Man and Levers Water. At the top end of the access road pass through a small gate next to a directional sign to the Y.H.A. on to a trackway. The track soon comes to a bridge which takes the track over Church Beck. (½ mile)

2   *Do not* cross over this bridge but keep to the left-hand side of Church Beck following an obvious pathway. Within a few hundred yards, after crossing over a stile, the path veers away from Church Beck towards the Old Man of Coniston. After climbing nearly 500 feet the path joins a trackway coming in from the left. (¾ mile)

3   Within 40 yards of joining this trackway another path leads off to the right. Be sure to *ignore* this turning and keep to the trackway, which makes a steep and twisting ascent through a complex series of abandoned quarry workings to the summit of the Old Man of Coniston. (1 mile)

4   From the summit head north along a graceful ridge to Swirl How. (1¾ miles)
    (In mist it is easy to mistake a path descending eastwards off Great How Crags for the path described below, or even for the path conti-nuing on to Swirl How. This is not a proper route and can lead one into serious difficulties. If you are therefore not certain of being on the summit of Swirl How you should return to the Old Man of Coniston.)

5   From the summit of Swirl How descend eastwards down to the gap between Swirl How and Wetherlam, and from thence ascend to the summit of Wetherlam itself. (1 mile)

6   From Wetherlam head south along a pleasant ridge path descending towards Coniston. Near to the 1,250 foot contour the path joins an old constructed mine path that leads down to an unsurfaced road-way running by the side of Church Beck. (1¾ miles)

7   Follow this unsurfaced road towards Coniston. Within a few hund-red yards on your right is the bridge which was bypassed at the start of the walk. Cross over the bridge now and return the way you previously came back to Coniston village. (¾ mile)

(As you return to Coniston village a very pleasing way to conclude this walk is to visit Dixon Ground Farm for a pot of tea. The farm is on your left just before reaching the Sun Hotel. It has an attractive small garden and very pleasant views overlooking the village and lake.)

THE FAIRFIELD HORSESHOE

Highest Point	Fairfield 2,863 feet
Distance	10½ miles
Total Ascent	3,150 feet
Average Time	6½ hours
Starting Point	*Ambleside Market Cross* (NY 376 046).

Exploring the streets of Ambleside the visitor will often glimpse a group of impressive and inviting hills lying to the north of the town. It is these hills that form the Fairfied Horseshoe.

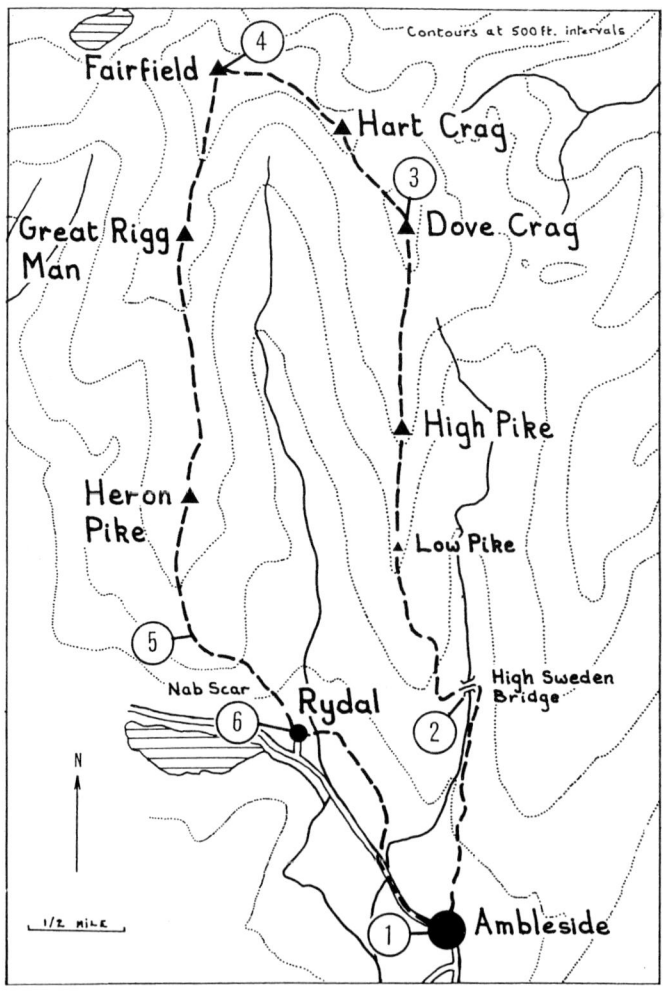

1   From the Market Cross walk up North Road, passing the Unicorn pub on your left, to a road junction. At the junction turn right and walk uphill. Take the first turn left into Sweden Bridge Lane. Belle Vue Lane soon branches off to the left. *Make sure to ignore this turning* and continue uphill. After a few hundred yards there is a fork in the road, bear left here along the clearly indicated continuation of Sweden Bridge Lane. Soon this becomes a very attractive enclosed trackway leading not surprisingly to High Sweden Bridge. (1¼ miles)

2   Cross over the bridge, pass through a small gate and turn left. The path climbs uphill and joins up with a more substantial path-cum-trackway. Follow this path northwards. After a short distance it reaches the crest of the ridge along which runs perhaps the most impressive wall in the Lake District. Continue along the path running along the side of this wall, over Low Pike and High Pike and on to Dove Crag, spot height 2,603 feet. (2¾ miles)

3   From here the path turns N.W. along the ridge over Hart Crag and on to Fairfield itself. (1½ miles)
    (The summit of Fairfield is quite flat, so to enjoy the best views possible spend some time exploring the northern and north eastern perimeters of the fell top.)

4   From the summit of Fairfield move south along a straight forward ridge path over Great Rigg Man and Heron Pike to the top of Nab Scar overlooking Rydal Water. (3 miles)

5   The following descent down to Rydal village is quite steep but has been made much easier by the recent work done on the path. (½ mile)

6   From Rydal village after passing Rydal Mount, the former home of Wordsworth, take the first turn left along an unsurfaced access road behind the very imposing looking Rydal Hall. Surprisingly this is a public right of way leading through the grounds of the Hall to the main road back to Ambleside. (1½ miles)

GREAT GABLE 2,949 feet

Distance	8 miles
Total Ascent	3,000 feet
Average Time	5¾ hours
Starting Point	*Seatoller Car Park* (NY 244 137).
Public Transport	Bus. Keswick to Seatoller. Service 79. Operators Cumberland.

Probably the noblest looking mountain in the Lake District, Great Gable looks impressive from every viewpoint. This walk ascends the mountain via the waterfall of Sour Milk Gill and the hanging valley of Gillercombe. On the summit you should easily locate a bronze plaque recording the purchase of Great Gable by the Fell and Rock Climbing Club in memory of the club members killed in the First World War.

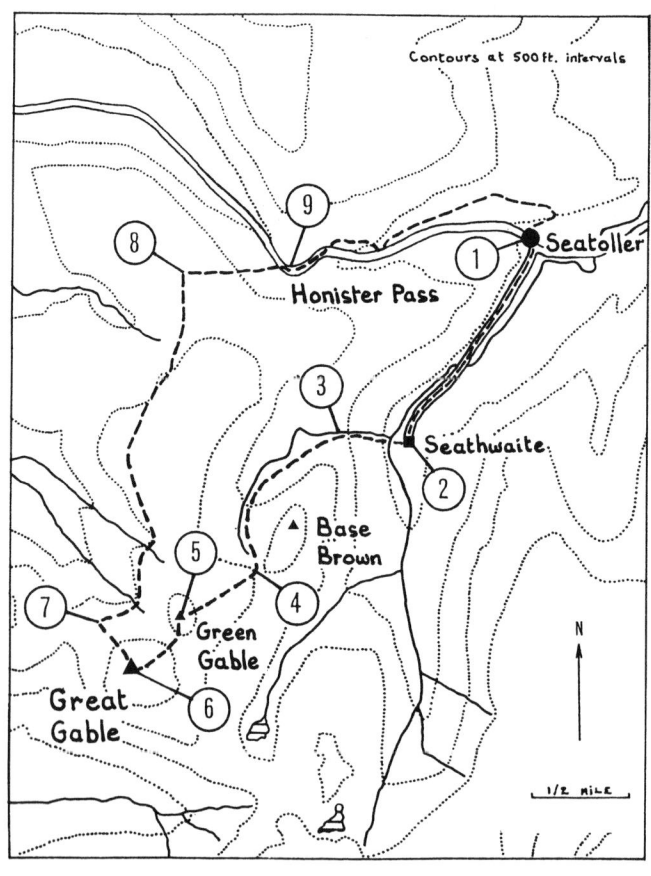

1   Walk from Seatoller along the road to Seathwaite. (1¼ miles)

2   Pass through the archway between the outbuildings of the farm along a short trackway and over a footbridge to the foot of Sour Milk Gill. To the left of the waterfall is a constructed path that leads to the top of the falls. (½ mile)

3   The path continues in to Gillercomb along the left hand side of the valley. Following the valley's main stream the path then climbs up to the saddle between Base Brown and Green Gable. (¾ mile)

4   From the saddle continue S.W. to the summit of Green Gable. (½ mile)

5   From Green Gable there is a short descent to Windy Gap followed by a final climb to the summit of Great Gable. (½ mile)
(A short walk of a hundred yards due S.W. from the summit will bring you to the Westmorland Cairn, generally considered to be the best viewpoint on Great Gable.)

6   From the summit head N.W. A steep descent soon develops. After descending roughly 700 feet the path comes on to a level section, a short truncated spur, over which crosses a line of iron posts, the remains of a former fence. (¼ mile)

7   From this point a path known as "Moses' Trod" leads off to the right initially following the line of the former fence. The path first moves eastwards traversing under the northern face of Great Gable to meet with the head waters of Ennerdale's river Liza. Crossing over the stream the path then heads in a northerly direction, roughly contouring around Green Gable, Brandreth and Grey Knotts, eventually to meet up with an old mineral line running from Dubs Quarry to Honister Pass. (2 miles)

8   The mineral line has long since become a path, therefore at this point turn right and follow the line down to the top of Honister Pass. (½ mile)

9   From the summit of Honister begin descending the road down to Seatoller. Within a quarter of a mile from the top of the pass notice a trackway leading off to the left. This is the original road and far better to follow. Within a short distance it will rejoin the present day road for a hundred yards but then it leads off to the left again. Nearing Seatoller it may seem as if the track will head away from Seatoller, but after seeming to by-pass the hamlet the track finally turns into it. You will certainly find the track far easier to follow than it is to follow its representation on the O.S. maps. (1¾ miles)

HELVELLYN 3,116 feet

Distance	9¼ miles
Total Ascent	3,000 feet
Average Time	6 hours
Starting Point	*Glenridding Car Park* (NY 386 170).

It is thought that Helvellyn is the most climbed mountain in the Lake District. It surpasses the magic figure of three thousand feet, which is achieved by only three other peaks in the Lake District. However, despite not being the highest mountain in the Lake District, Helvellyn is more accessible than Scafell Pike and Scafell, the two peaks which are higher, so consequently it is climbed more. The ascent taken in this walk is via Striding Edge, a sharp, dramatic, serrated ridge which is no doubt the most difficult route to the summit but because of its qualities has become the most popular. There are no less than four memorials passed by on this walk. One memorial that doesn't exist but perhaps should, is to Tommy Hodgson, a Keswickian, who in his retirement years, until well into his eighties, ascended Helvellyn well over two hundred times.

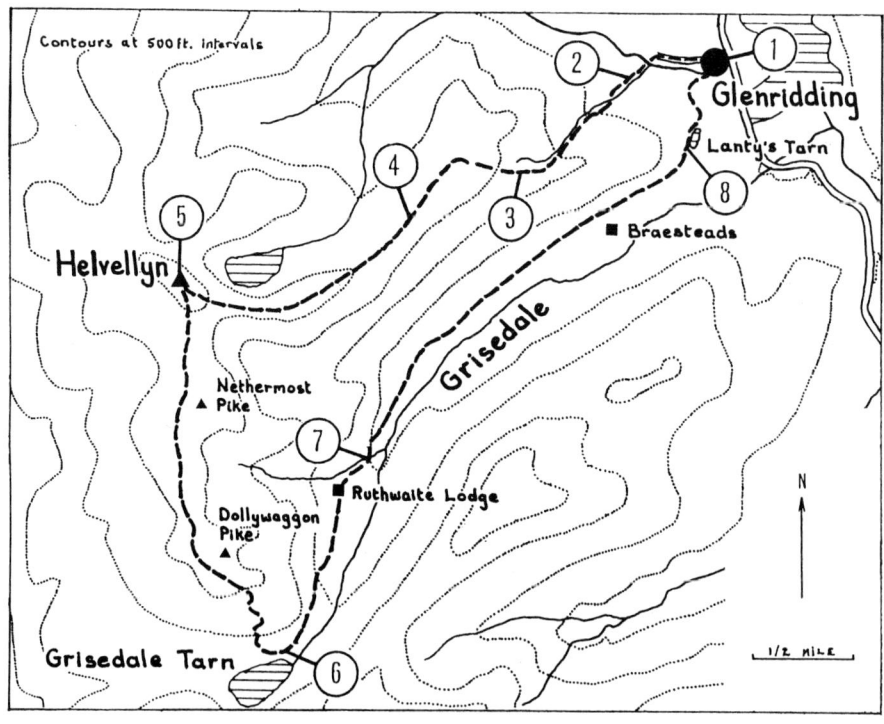

1   From the Information Centre, following the footpath direction signs, exit from the western end of the car park next to the Health Centre on to a roadway. Turn left and follow the road uphill. Where the road bends an access road branches off to the left to Gillside Farm. Follow this access road over a bridge and uphill, making sure not to turn left into the farm, but to continue uphill to a five bar farm gate. (½ mile)

2   Continue through the gate and uphill for another hundred yards. At this point branching off to the right is a distinct path sign posted as leading to "Helvellyn via Mires Beck". Follow this path a few hundred yards uphill to a gate and a stile. Pass through the gate and turn left to continue along the path following Mires Beck. The path climbs steeply uphill eventually joining at roughly 1,700 feet a solid ridge wall. (¾ mile)

3   The path continues along the ridge following the wall. After climbing a few hundred feet a dramatic sight of Helvellyn and Catstycam comes into view. There now follows a welcome level section still following the wall to where the wall makes a sharp left hand bend and the path joins another path ascending from Grisedale. (¾ mile)

4   The path continues along the ridge on to Striding Edge itself. Outside the winter season there is no great difficulty to Striding Edge. The most exciting way to cross it is to keep to the actual crest of the ridge, but there is an easier path if needed just below the crest of the ridge on the right hand side. The most difficult part comes where the ridge descends sharply before the final climb to the summit, but this is no more than a scramble. On reaching the summit ridge turn right to walk the last few hundred yards to the summit marked by a triangulation pillar. (1¼ miles)

5   From the summit walk south along a very clear ridge path. Half a mile from the summit another path branches off to the right which descends down to Wythburn, make sure to ignore this and keep to the higher path. Better views still are obtainable by ignoring the path altogether and walking along the actual edge of the ridge, and rejoining the main path at the col between Nethermost Pike and Dollywaggon Pike. Should you do this in winter make sure you are properly equipped. Finally the path descends the southern face of Dollywaggon to join up with an old packhorse route near the outflow of Grisedale Tarn. (2 miles)

6   Follow the old packhorse route northwards into Grisedale. After descending 500 feet the path comes to Ruthwaite Lodge. A few hundred yards on from the hut on your left is a footbridge. (1 mile)

7   Cross over the footbridge and follow the path on the other side which contours along the northern side of the valley. After passing above Braesteads Farm the path begins a steady 200 foot climb to Lanty's Tarn, passing through a kissing gate at the point where it is crossed by the path ascending up to Striding Edge. (2½ miles)

8   From Lanty's Tarn an obvious path descends northwards to Glenridding. (½ mile)

HIGH STREET 2,719 feet

Distance	9 miles
Total Ascent	2,400 feet
Average Time	5½ hours
Starting Point	*Hartsop* (NY 410 131). A car park is sited at the top end of the village.

High Street is so named after the Roman road which once traversed the long range of hills that runs from Windermere to Pooley Bridge, of which High Street is the highest point. These are much gentler hills compared to the more rugged fells to the west. The descent is via Angle Tarn, probably the most appealing tarn in the Lake District, because of its open setting. The top of High Street itself is very broad and almost flat, so much so it once had a race course!

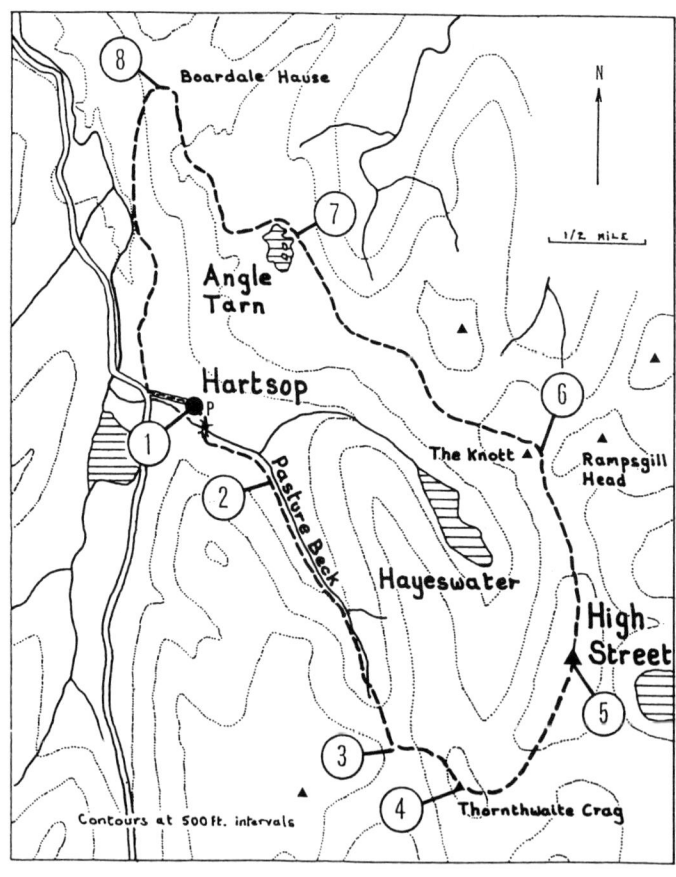

1 Exit Hartsop car park through the kissing gate at its eastern edge and immediately turn right down to a bridge and continue on the distinct path ahead of you to another five bar gate. Pass through the gate and turn left. Follow the path along the wall into Pasture Beck valley. (½ mile)

2 The path along the valley is lightly used compared with other Lakeland paths but is still easy enough to follow. A final steep climb at the head of the valley brings you to Threshthwaite Mouth, the col between Stony Cove Pike and Thornthwaite Crag. (1½ miles)

3 From the top of the col take the steep climb to your left up to Thornthwaite Crag. Follow the wall at the top of the ridge S.E. to an extremely tall cairn or beacon marking the summit. (½ mile)

4 From Thornthwaite Crag a very obvious path curves north-eastwards round the head of Hayeswater valley onto High Street to within a few yards of the summit marked by a large white triangulation pillar involving less than 200 feet of climbing. (1 mile)

5 From the summit of High Street follow the stone wall crossing over the fell northwards. After ¾ mile a path veers off to the right. *Ignore* this path and keep to the path following the wall. This will bring you to a small gap between The Knott and Rampsgill Head. (1 mile)

6 The path moves around The Knott and begins descending in a north-westerly direction. Be careful not to take a path branching off this path that descends down to Hayeswater though it is much less distinct. After crossing over a beck the path heads towards Angle Tarn roughly keeping to the 1,750 foot contour. (1¾ miles)

7 The path continues around the northern edge of Angle Tarn and then leads northwards to Boardale Hause, the gap between Place Fell and Angle Tarn Pikes. (1 mile)

8 From Boardale Hause the path continues down to Patterdale village. Follow this path a short way to a point where surprisingly a cast iron pipe emerges out of the ground emitting a refreshing trickle of water, at this point a less distinct path veers off to the left. Follow this path down to the foot of the fell where it joins a trackway leading back to Hartsop village and the start of the walk. (1¾ miles)

THE NEWLANDS HORSESHOE

Highest Point	Dale Head 2,473 feet
Distance	10 1/2 miles
Total Ascent	3,500 feet
Average Time	7 hours
Starting Point	A) *Hawes End Landing* (NY 251 213) or
	B) *Gutherscale Car Park* (NY 247 212).
	Launch. Keswick Boat Landing to Hawes End
	Landing. Operators Keswick Launch Company.

This walk is a very undulating circuit around one of Lakeland's more pastoral valleys. The walk has four separate distinct ascents and descents. Car owners may prefer to start at directional note 8 where there is a small car park, to avoid the slight ascent at the finish.

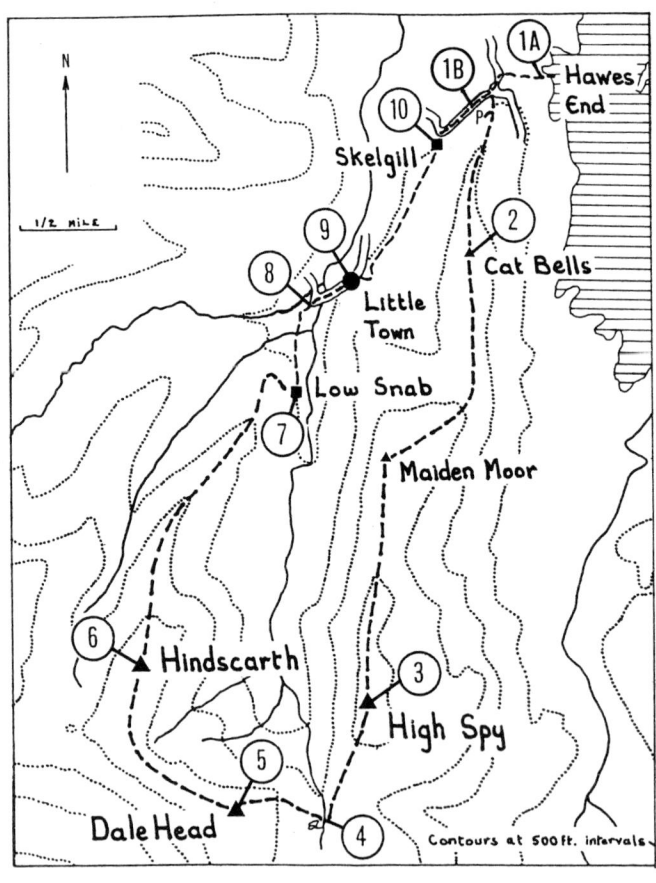

1A From Hawes End Landing walk uphill along a distinctive path across an unsurfaced driveway and on to the Portinscale to Grange road. Continue uphill over a cattle-grid for 100 yards to a sharp hairpin bend where there is also a road junction. From the corner of the junction is an obvious constructed, though unsigned, pathway which leads to the summit of Cat Bells. (1 mile)

1B From Gutherscale car park is a clearly constructed path way sign posted as leading to the summit of Cat Bells. (1 mile)

2 From the summit of Cat Bells continue south, descending at first 250 feet then ascending along a clearly defined path on to Maiden Moor and then on to High Spy. (2½ miles)

3 From High Spy the path descends southwards veering to the right away from the line of the ridge down towards a deep set stream flowing into Newlands. The path crosses over the stream and climbs up to Dale Head Tarn. (¾ mile)

4 The path moves round the northern side of the tarn (not as the O.S. map indicates the southern side) and climbs up to the summit of Dale Head. The path is very ill-defined at times and easily lost, but it is always clear where you should be going, that is straight uphill. If you have problems locating the path you should have no problems locating the summit. (½ mile)

5 From Dale Head continue north westwards along a well defined ridge path descending some few hundred feet. Just as the path begins to ascend once more a thinner path veers off to the right which leads to the summit of Hindscarth. (1 mile)

6 Continue northwards from the summit of Hindscarth descending down an ever narrowing ridge, eventually arriving at Low Snab Farm. (1½ miles)

7 Follow the farm access road past Newland's church to a gated road junction. (½ mile)
(Walkers using public transport and interested in returning to Keswick other than by launch should here turn left and walk up the road to Rigg Beck, a large purple house, where they can catch the Mountain Goat minibus back to Keswick. Seasonal only.)

8 Turn right and walk up the road to Little Town. (¼ mile)

9 Walk through the hamlet. 25 yards after passing a post box on your right is the start of a trackway leading to East Ho. From here there is a fairly traceable right of way mainly following a line of hawthorn bushes across a series of fields to Skelgill Farm. (1 mile)

10 From here follow the road north-eastwards to Gutherscale car park (¼ mile) or its junction with the Portinscale Grange road and thence to Hawes End boat landings. (½ mile)

PILLAR 2,927 feet

Distance	9½ miles
Total Ascent	3,300 feet
Average Time	6½ hours
Starting Point	*Overbeck Bridge* (NY 168 068). Car park adjacent to the bridge.

Beginning from Lakeland's most majestic valley this walk to the summit of Pillar is via the High Level Route, possibly the most adventurous mile of path in the Lake District. The path is ascribed to John Tyson Robinson, an early rock climbing pioneer who developed the path as a way of reaching Pillar Rock, which was then, and still is, a major rock climbing crag. Robinson's cairn was built in his memory. On reaching it Pillar Rock comes fully into view.

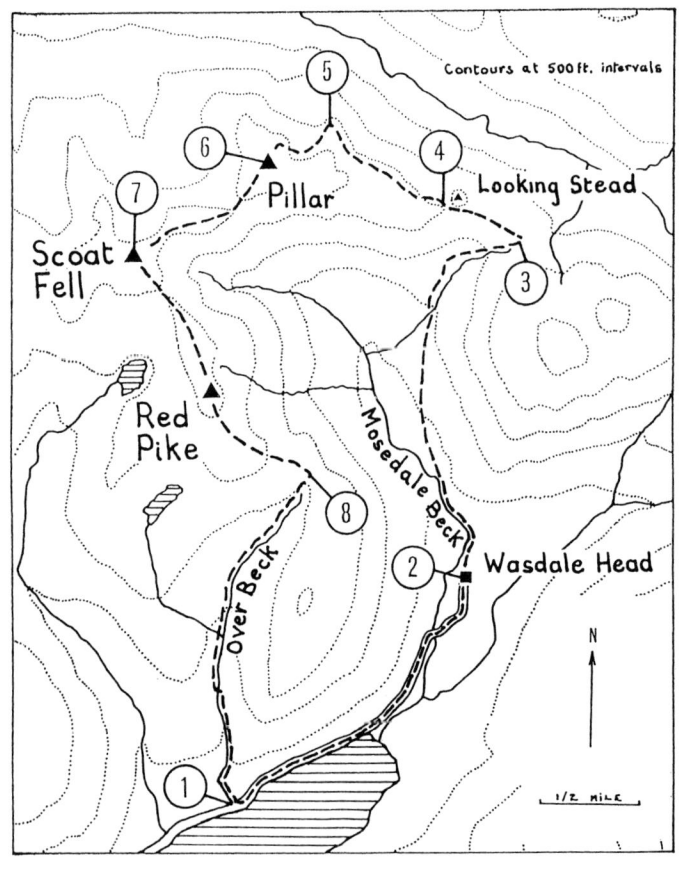

26

1 Follow the road N.E. to the Wasdale Head Inn at the head of the valley. (1¾ miles)

2 Behind the hotel follow a path next to the river, Mosedale Beck. *Do not* cross over the bridge. After passing through a five-bar gate the path follows the side of a wall into Mosedale itself. This is an old pack horse route and climbs to the top of Black Sail Pass. (2 miles)

3 From the top of the pass turn left, N.W., and follow the ridge to a small saddle between Looking Stead, a rounded hillock which you pass on your right, and the shoulder of Pillar. (½ mile)

4 From the saddle the simplest way to the summit of Pillar is to follow the ridge. More interesting however is the High Level Route. To locate the somewhat elusive start of this route begin climbing the ridge, but only a hundred feet or so. Look carefully at each cairn. From one particular cairn leading away to your right is a narrow path. This is the start of the High Level Route, which descends, slightly to begin with, then delicately traverses the northern face of Pillar to Robinson's Cairn placed prominently on a distinctive knoll. (¾ mile)

5 From Robinson's Cairn the path is obvious enough even if the terrain seems daunting. The path descends then ascends a steep scree slope, from the top of which it moves out right across a tilted slab, the Shamrock Traverse, bringing you to a point overlooking Pillar Rock. From here the path ascends a steep ridge to the summit of Pillar. (½ mile)

6 From the summit head S.W. down to Wind Gap and then along the ridge to Scoat Fell. (¾ mile)

7 From Scoat Fell head S.E. along the ridge, visiting Red Pike, and descending down to Dore Head. (1½ miles)

8 From Dore Head move S.W. in to Over Beck valley, keeping to the western side of the stream. Though this path is indicated on the map there is little evidence of it on the ground until you come to a stream flowing from Low Tarn. You now seem assured of an easy path back but this is not so. The path leads to a wall through which there is no right of way. You must therefore follow the wall down to a footbridge crossing over Over Beck itself. The path on the other side of the footbridge is obvious but quite narrow. It follows the final section of Over Beck back to the car park. (2 miles)

SCAFELL 3,162 feet

Distance	9 miles
Total Ascent	3,000 feet
Average Time	6 hours
Starting Point	*Foot of Hard Knott Pass* (NY 212 012). Verge side parking is possible along the road leading to the foot of the pass.

This walk passes through the most mountainous scenery in Cumbria. The ascent route along the side of the river Esk is the finest ascent in the Lake District and possesses several entrancing revelations. Scafell though is no place for getting disorientated in mist, as it is bounded by some precipitous cliffs; good navigational skills therefore are essential.

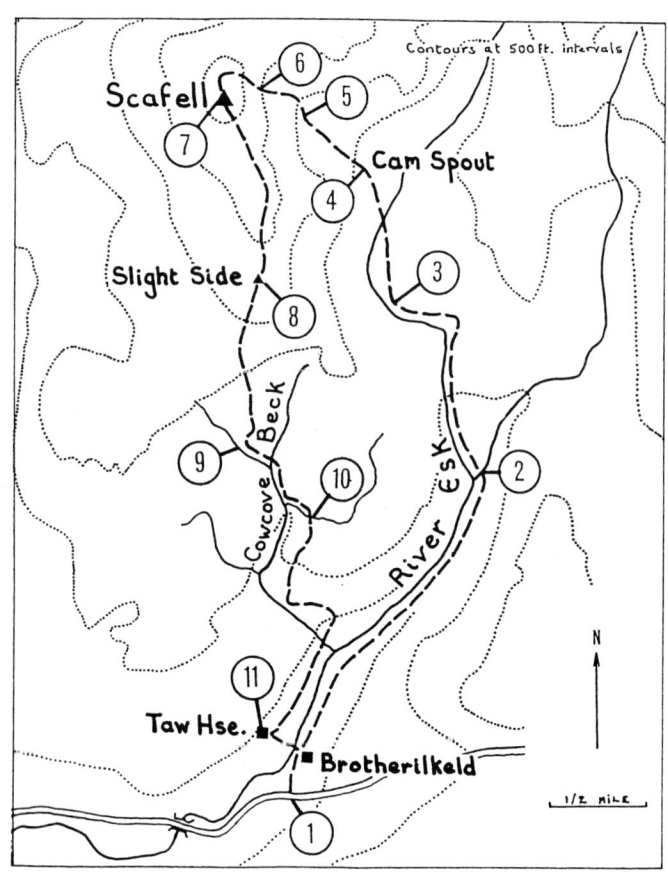

1   From the foot of Hard Knott Pass walk along the access road to Brotherilkeld Farm. Before entering the farm the path branches off left to follow the river's edge. After passing through a gateway the path crosses two large fields and then continues up the valley following the river Esk to a small packhorse bridge. (2 miles)

2   Cross over the bridge. Still following the Esk the path begins a steep climb, but after passing through a miniature gorge the terrain dramatically levels and the river takes a large curve westwards. The path continues along the side of the river following its westward course, but in little more than a quarter of a mile the course of the river alters yet again and a wide spacious area comes in view. (1 mile)

3   This is the area of Great Moss. Immediately ahead of you is the extensive and impressive rock face of Cam Spout Crags. At the northern end of these crags is a waterfall. This is Cam Spout itself, after which the crags are named. Head for the base of this waterfall fording the river Esk to do so. (¾ mile)

4   To the right of the waterfall is a steep scramble. This is actually the start of the path which leads to Mickledore, the gap between Scafell and Scafell Pike. Follow this route until you come to the start of a boulder field, 500 to 600 feet from the top of Mickledore itself. (¾ mile)

5   After climbing roughly 200 feet from the start of the boulder field you should observe on your left a deep narrow gully. Though something of a scramble this is the route to Foxes Tarn. You should find clear signs of its usage as you climb it. (¼ mile)

6   From Foxes Tarn the path continues up a scree slope to the summit ridge of Scafell. On reaching the top of the ridge turn left to reach the summit. (¼ mile)

7   From the summit of Scafell follow the ridge south to Slight Side. (1 mile)

8   Follow a cairned path descending off Slight Side till you come to a swift flowing stream, the first real beck you come across on your descent from Scafell. Nearby, next to the stream, are the remains of a dead tree, which are so distinctive you should have no doubt about having located the correct stream. (¾ mile)

9   Follow the beck down to its junction with Cowcove Beck. Then follow Cowcove Beck down stream a couple of hundred yards to where another tributary, Damas Dubs, flows in from the left. Now follow this tributary up stream a few hundred yards to a footbridge created out of two sheets of corrugated iron. (½ mile)

10 Follow the path crossing over the footbridge southwards. The path is part of a constructed route way, probably a former peat road, that leads gracefully down to Taw House Farm. (1¼ miles)

11 From Taw House Farm a path leads to a footbridge crossing over the river Esk and back to the start of the walk. (¼ mile)

SCAFELL PIKE 3,206 feet

Distance	8 miles
Total Ascent	3,100 feet
Average Time	5¾ hours
Starting Point	*Seathwaite* (NY 235 122). Car parking is possible along the road verge leading to the hamlet.
Public Transport	Bus. Keswick to Seatoller (1¼ miles distance from Seathwaite). Service 79. Operators Cumberland.

The summit of Scafell Pike is, of course, the highest point in England. It is also an excellent fell walk, particularly the ascent to the summit via the Corridor Route, which is the approach chosen in this walk.

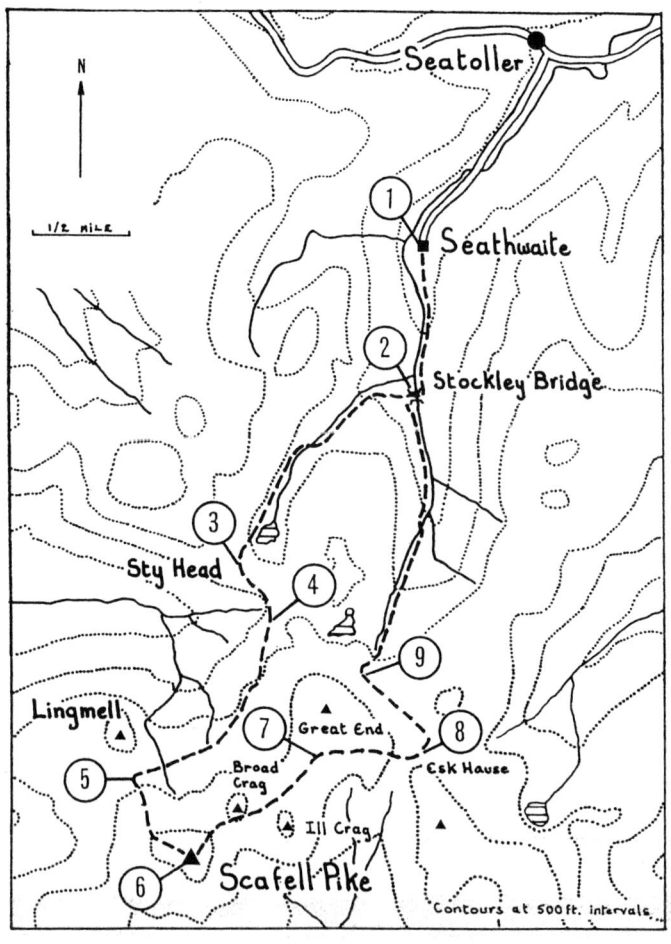

30

1   From Seathwaite farm walk along a clear trackway up the valley to Stockley Bridge. (¾ mile)

2   Cross over the bridge through the gate and straight on up the hillside towards a group of conifer trees. This is an old pack horse route and leads first to Styhead Tarn and then, a ¼ mile further on, to Styhead Pass itself. (1½ miles)

3   Locate a well known First Aid Stretcher Box sited next to a large boulder at the summit of the pass. Look due S.E., a quarter of a mile away on Great End is a deep ravine, Skew Gill. Head for the base of this ravine. There is no path to begin with but after a hundred yards or so a path should become evident. (¼ mile)

4   The Corridor Route begins from the base of Skew Gill, climbing out of the gill (a slight scramble) and leading quite clearly up to the col between Lingmell and Scafell Pike itself. (1¼ miles)

5   From the col climb S.E. up the ridge to the summit of Scafell Pike. (½ mile)

6   Head N.E. from the summit. This is rough ground but along a well worn path, a steep descent to begin with, then over Broad Crag and across Ill Crag to the col between Ill Crag and Great End. (¾ mile)

7   From the col the path moves eastwards and descends down to Esk Hause, the saddle between Great End and Esk Pike. A short way N.E. of Esk Hause is a windbreak, two walls in the form of a cross. (½ mile)

8   A hundred yards N.E. of the windbreak a reddish path turns sharply to the north-west, in the direction of Great Gable if it is visible, running parallel to a deep ravine. Follow the path until you come to a distinctive piece of cobbled path crossing over the beck running through the ravine. (½ mile)

9   Cross over the beck and continue along an obvious path which soon descends northwards along Grains Gill down to Stockley Bridge. From there retrace your steps back to Seathwaite. (2¼ miles)

SAFETY ON THE FELLS

Clothing:
Waterproof/windproof outer jacket.
Sturdy boots with a good sole pattern.
Hat and gloves and spare warm clothing - even in summer it can be cold on the tops.

Equipment:
Comfortable day sack.
Food and something to drink.
Compass.
Torch - in case you are overtaken by darkness.
Whistle - for attracting attention if you get into difficulties.
Large polybag - to shelter in in extremis.

Winter Walking:
In icy conditions it is very advisable to carry an ice axe.

Leave details of your route with someone before you set off but be prepared to modify your plans if you have to. For a weather forecast of fell top conditions phone 017687 75757.

PUBLIC TRANSPORT

There are public transport connections to the starting point of all the walks in this guide save for the Pillar and Scafell walks though some are only seasonal. Nine of the connections are operated by Cumberland Motors (01946 63222) and one by the Derwentwater Launch company (017687 72263).

Cumbria County Council also provide a comprehensive information service 'Journey Planner' which can advise how to travel between any two points in the county - 01228 606000.

June, 1998.